PERFECT PEACE

DAILY DEVOTIONAL

OVERCOMING ANXIETY, FEAR, AND
WORRY TO WALK IN THE
UNSHAKABLE PEACE OF GOD

31 Days to Establish the Perfect Peace of God in Your
Heart and Mind

BY

CLAY BROOKS

ISBN-13: 978-0-9849271-1-1

Unless otherwise indicated, all Scripture quotations in this book are from the New American Standard Version of the Bible.

DEDICATION

I dedicate this devotional to my Lord Jesus Christ, the Prince of Peace, who took all my worries and fears onto Himself, on the cross, so that I could be set free and walk in perfect peace through all the storms, trials, and tribulations of life. I love You, Lord.

"But he was being punished for what we did. He was crushed because of our guilt. He took the punishment we deserved, and this brought us peace. We were healed because of his pain" (**Isaiah 53:5**). (ERV)

ACKNOWLEDGEMENTS

I want to thank Pastor Rod Aguillard, Senior Overseer of the Network of Related Pastors for his encouragement, input and insight on the manuscript and final proof of this book. He has written six books, and his help was key in making needed improvements before going to print.

I also want to acknowledge my wife, Anita, for her skills and hard work in helping me put this devotional together. She is a beautiful "helpmeet" and gift from God who has supported and undergirded me in fulfilling the things God has called us to do together.

FOREWARD

Clay is a man of great faith. He has been molded, tested, and tried through the fires of adversity and warfare. His heart to see the nations come to know the Lord Jesus Christ has sent him and his family to many lands to share the gospel with unreached people groups.

In <u>Perfect Peace Daily Devotional</u> there is a beautiful, deep flow of the Holy Spirit to bring the Lord's peace, freedom, refreshing, and grace. While many are struggling in our world with fear and uncertainty, the Lord desires to establish a people of His Kingdom who are sons and daughters of righteousness, peace, and joy in the Holy Spirit.

Our Father God is a God of deep compassions, tender mercies, and unshakable peace. May your heart open to the impartations of Who He is, His goodness, and establish peace and victory through the pages of this book.

In His Peace,
Ruthie Brooks Rose

INTRODUCTION

SCRIPTURAL MEDITATIONS FOR EACH DAY
OF THE MONTH THAT BRING PEACE, AND
DELIVERANCE FROM WORRY AND FEAR.

This book was written to be a companion to my previous book "Fear No Evil." I had learned that particular, guided, daily meditation in the Word of God is a key to walking in peace, and being set free from tormenting anxiety and fear. I felt the Lord lead me to write this devotional to give you, the reader, a daily meal of meditations from God's Word to strengthen your spirit and renew your thoughts. This book is like a doctor's prescription with thirty-one tablets to be taken one per day for thirty-one days. They are also like scriptural, daily vitamins to boost your spiritual immune system. There are thirty-one meditations, one for each day of the month.

The Bible is a collection of the thoughts, words, and actions of God. His thoughts and words created the Garden of Eden, the paradise of God. His thoughts and words were all there in the Garden in the beginning. As long as Adam and Eve believed and obeyed His thoughts and words, there was perfect peace, joy, and love. It was the interjection of strange, contradictory, and deceptive words from the serpent that brought the first attack against Eve. Only when Eve began to consider and entertain those insidious, seductive words of the devil did her peaceful paradise become threatened. And amazingly, she was seemingly unaware of the seriousness of the situation as the future of the human race hung in the balance.

This action against Eve and Adam was a premeditated spiritual attack. The devil was attacking the godly, scriptural way of thinking that God had given them. So we must realize that *our* right thoughts will be challenged, ridiculed and attacked as well. Of course, any wrong ways of thinking we may already have can be rooted out by meditating on God's Word. Meditating daily on the Word of God is one of the scriptural disciplines, habits, and joys that we must build into our lives if we ever hope to live victoriously over fear, worry, or any other attack of the enemy.

When the devil tempted Jesus, he tempted Him also with deceptive and seductive thoughts and words. Jesus responded with "It is written." He counterattacked with God's thoughts and words. He worked at, and fought to keep the right thoughts and words, the words of God. He even said that our very life was wrapped up in hearing, receiving, and knowing God's thoughts and words. He said, "Man doesn't live by bread alone, but by every word that proceeds from the mouth of God" (**Matthew 4:4**).

We are to be like Jesus. He knew the Word of God. He believed and used it against demonic attack. He said, "It is written!" We must do this too. Finally, He told the devil to "Begone!" We can and should do this as well. For example, we can say, "Lord, You said in **Mark 16** that, in Your name,

I would cast out demons of fear, panic, and terror. So I command fear to go now, in Jesus' name."

Enough cannot be said about the importance of meditating on the words and thoughts of God every day, and throughout the day. Here in this devotional are some of the Scriptures that have helped me get set free from fear and maintain the peace of God in my life.

There will be certain verses that seem to encourage you personally more than others. Concentrate on those verses. Learn and memorize them. Meditate on them and use them in your daily prayer times and throughout the day. That is how you will practice living in the peace that comes "by every word that proceeds from the mouth of God." "Every word" also includes those specific words that the Holy Spirit makes real and alive to you personally. Scriptures about some other subject are beneficial, to be sure, but they probably won't help give peace and rest to your spirit and mind as much as these scriptures that specifically deal with bringing peace to your life.

Speak the Scriptures out loud as you meditate on them. Personalize them by praying and declaring them to be true in your life. Your faith will grow, and the peace of God will begin to fill your heart and mind like the calm, crystal sea before the throne of God.

You will keep him in perfect peace, whose mind is stayed on you..." **Isaiah 26:3** (AKJV)

Day 1

Meditation Brings Peace

Psalm 1:1-3 – "How blessed is the man who does not walk in the counsel of the wicked, Nor stand in the path of sinners, Nor sit in the seat of scoffers!

2 But his delight is in the law of the LORD, And in His law he **meditates** day and night.

3 He will be like a tree *firmly* planted by streams of water, Which yields its fruit in its season And its leaf does not wither; And in whatever he does, he prospers."

It is one of the devil's best-kept secrets. He has deceived Christians so well that most of us think it's something for only Buddhists and New Age people to do. What is this secret, godly practice that guarantees success wherever you go, and prosperity in whatever you do? Sadly and tragically, it's what most Christians have not been taught to do. It is what the Bible simply calls **meditation,** meditation on God's Word (**Joshua 1, Psalm 1**).

What you meditate on, what you think about every day, not only will determine your level of success in life, but will also be a major factor in determining whether or not you overcome fear, grow in faith, and walk in the peace of God. That is the reason why I put this passage on day one. Meditation in the Word of God is an essential part of a true disciple of Jesus Christ's daily life. Why is meditation on the Word of God so beneficial? Because when you meditate on and then begin to believe God's thoughts and promises, it builds and strengthens your faith, and strong faith will naturally overcome fear and worry. Also, what you meditate on, you will be much more likely to do and obey. And obedience is the goal of meditation. For it is obedience that is pleasing to God and brings the blessings of God.

For some years on the mission field, I struggled with different fears and worries. But when I began to meditate on God's truth and His promises related to those specific fears, I found that most of them just melted away like snow on a warm, spring day. They were gone! They just disappeared by the power of the Word. There is power in meditating on the Word of God. And meditating is more than just reading. It is pondering, and thinking about something over and over. It is asking God to reveal to you truth out of the Scriptures. When we do this, it helps the Word of God enter our spirit, where faith grows and will work for us.

• •

Prayer Declaration – Lord, I thank You for the Word of God. I will meditate on Your Word today. I will not meditate or think on the devil's thoughts of fear, failure, worry, and doubt. I will not "walk in the counsel of the wicked." I will walk in Your counsel today. I delight in Your Word. I meditate on Your Words day and night. So I will be like a tree firmly planted by streams of water. I will yield good fruit. My leaves will not wither, and in whatever I do, I will prosper. Thank You, Lord.

Day 2

He Is With You

Genesis 28:15 - "Behold, I am with you and will keep you wherever you go, and will bring you back to this land; for I will not leave you until I have done what I have promised you."

In December of 1985, my wife, two-year-old and one-month-old daughters, and I had moved to Montana to pastor a church among the Cheyenne Native Americans. Soon after arriving, we drove to Miles City to get snow tires. On the desolate way back, in the middle of nowhere, our vehicle overheated. It was getting dark, and the temperature was below freezing. Then it began to snow. The situation was turning from bad to worse. Anita and I began to call out to the Lord in prayer and ask Him to help us.

I rolled the car down the hill and saw house lights in the distance. We made it to the ranch, but no one was answering the door. Finally, when I was turning around to go back to the car, a young lady, who was alone inside, slowly opened the door. I explained our dilemma, and she mercifully welcomed us all in. Thank God!

Her father, Mr. Moffitt, arrived shortly and helped us call a tow truck, 18 miles back in Miles City, to come get us (No cell phones back then). As we waited for the truck, they gave us hot chocolate and warmed us by their fire. Later, as we crammed into the tow truck to ride back to Miles City in the snow, we thanked God for His faithfulness and His promises that He would "be with us and protect us wherever we went."

God spoke these verses in Genesis we read today to Jacob, but He also says the same thing to us today through Jesus Christ and the New Covenant. He makes this promise to us if we love Him and follow Him closely.

If you are traveling or moving to another city or country, knowing that God will be with you is of utmost importance. I know. I have been there. I've moved to and lived in several countries around the world. God tells us here in these verses that not only will He be with us, but will also protect us wherever we go in obedience to Him. Sometimes people have questioned the wisdom of where I was taking my family to live. But actually, the safest place we can ever be is in the center of the will of God, no matter where that may be. Thank God we are never alone.

• •

Prayer Declaration – Lord, I thank You that You are with me today wherever I go. I am blessed going out and coming back in, in Jesus' name. I will remember this promise and not forget that wherever I go, we go together. I will talk with You throughout this day because we'll be together. Your presence is becoming more real to me than the people around me, in Jesus' name. I thank You that I am never alone, and never abandoned. Hallelujah!

Day 3

Angelic Peace

Exodus 23:20 - "Behold, I am going to send an angel before you to guard you along the way and to bring you into the place which I have prepared.

Matthew 18:10 "See that you do not despise one of these little ones, for I say to you that **their angels** in heaven continually see the face of My Father who is in heaven.

Did you know that your angel does not leave you just because you grow up? They "camp around those who fear the Lord" (**Psalm 34:7**).

My wife, our five children, and I were at Guangzhou train station, Guangdong Province, China, and found out that we had to go to *another* train station in the city to catch our next train. We barely had time to make it. To make matters worse, we didn't know how to get there.

A young man walked up to us and asked if he could help. He explained what we needed to do, took us to the taxi stand and helped us get a taxi. I was so surprised by how helpful he was and that he even left the train station to help us find the taxi to where we needed to go. So I thanked him, and he responded, "Oh, this is what I am supposed to do. I am a soldier in the People's Liberation Army." I was totally shocked by what he said. My mind was rapidly trying to comprehend what I had just heard as he left and we drove off. The People's Liberation Army is the army of Communist China. I never expected to hear a PLA soldier say such a thing or be so helpful. I began to have the distinct feeling and sense that he was an angel sent to help us. He was one of God's "liberation angels" that the Lord sent to meet our need at just the right time.

Following the same theme, God encouraged Moses and the people of Israel by assuring them that *His angel* would also go with them. We, as well, can take comfort in this verse if we believe it.

How do we appropriate the faith and comfort that this verse can bring when we go to work, travel away from home, or just live our daily lives? I would personalize this verse in prayer. I would say, "Lord, I believe You and thank You that Your angel is with me, and goes before me to prepare the way, and give me success."

• •

Prayer Declaration – Lord, I thank You for my angel. I also thank You for the angels around me because I fear You. I thank You for their protection and that they guard my family and me. I am walking in Your will for my life, so I thank You that angels even protect me from injury and hitting my foot against a stone, in Jesus' name (**Psalm 91**).

Day 4

Following the Shepherd of Our Peace

Psalm 23:1-4 – "The LORD is my shepherd, I shall not want.

2 He makes me lie down in green pastures; He leads me beside quiet waters.

3 He restores my soul; He guides me in the paths of righteousness For His name's sake.

4 Even though I walk through the valley of the shadow of death, I fear no evil, for You are with me; Your rod and Your staff, they comfort me.

In 1736 John Wesley, founder of the Methodist Church, was on a ship bound for America. Traveling on board was also a contingency of Moravian missionaries. Wesley was greatly impressed by their disciplined consecration, and their humility in the way they served the other passengers and did things for them which none of the English would do. Some of the passengers on board mistreated them cruelly, and even struck and knocked some of them down, but they wouldn't hit back or get offended.

"Then, one day, a great storm broke over the ship, and everyone's perception of the Moravians changed. When the main sail split and the sea began to pour into the ship, the English panicked as terrible screams rose through the tumult of the storm. The Moravians sat quietly singing their hymns in perfect peace. Afterwards, when asked if they were not afraid, one of the Moravians answered, 'I thank God, no.' Then he was asked if their women and children were afraid and he replied, 'No, our women and children are not afraid to die.'"

Wesley recorded the following in his diary: "From them (the Moravians) I went to their crying, trembling neighbors, and pointed out to them the difference in the hour of trial, between him that fear God, and him that fears not. At twelve the wind fell. This was the most glorious day which I have hitherto seen." (http://www.christianitytoday.com/history/issues/issue- 1/moravians-and-john-wesley.html)

Probably no other passage of Scripture has helped people with fear and worry as much as the 23rd Psalm. I'm sure these Moravian missionaries knew it by heart and had meditated on it many times. They had meditated on these verses until they knew the Shepherd, and that He would rescue them when they called upon Him. And as a result, the Lord was honored through their lives and they made a strong impression on Wesley. He knew that he didn't know the Lord the way these Moravians did. And it made him hungry for the spiritual life and relationship with God that they had.

In verse four, the "valley of the shadow death" can be translated "valley of deep darkness." So this valley is a place where fear tries to breed. Many times we experience fear because we are alone or feel alone. But when someone else is with us, we may not experience fear at all or at least feel it to a much lesser degree. So when we fully embrace and have true belief that God, our Father, is with us at all times, a supernatural peace will guard our hearts and minds even in very dark, scary times or places.

Prayer Declaration – Lord, I thank You that You are my Shepherd. I follow You. I will follow Your leading today. I will walk in Your paths of righteousness and peace. And in Jesus' name, even though I go through dark times, I will fear no evil because I know that You are with me. I believe more and more that You are with me and therefore I am never alone.

Day 5

The Lord Is My Defense

Psalm 27:1-3 – "The LORD is my light and my salvation; Whom shall I fear? The LORD is the defense of my life; Whom shall I dread?

2 When evildoers came upon me to devour my flesh, My adversaries and my enemies, they stumbled and fell.

3 Though a host encamp against me, My heart will not fear; Though war arise against me, In *spite of* this I shall be confident.

My wife Anita and I were missionaries in Russia for three years ('92-'95), planting churches right after it opened up. The economy was in a shambles, and life was pretty tough for most Russians. There was a lot of drunkenness, and alcoholism was taking hold of more and more people as they turned to drink to help them cope with the fear and uncertainty of those days.

One Sunday, while living in Izhevsk, I ordered a taxi to come and take Anita, our four kids, and one of our co-workers, Janie Latiolais Sotillo, to our service an hour later. As they were getting into the vehicle, two drunk men came up and decided that they wanted the taxi instead. The driver explained that my wife had ordered the taxi and so he couldn't take them. But they wouldn't take no for an answer. At first, they were just arguing, but then a two-drunk-men-against-one-sober-taxi-driver fistfight broke out. Anita wasn't sure whether to get the kids out and leave or what. Of course, they were alarmed by what was happening and began to call out to the Lord. The Lord heard their cry, and pretty soon the driver beat them back enough to get into the taxi and try to leave. But as he was trying to pull away, one of the men stumbled over and gave one last jab that caught the driver just over the eye, opening a bloody cut. As they drove away, they all breathed a sigh of relief. Anita told him where they were going, and paid him extra for what he had done and gone through to take them. We all thanked the Lord for His promises and faithfulness to protect His children.

In **Psalm 27** we see the Lord provides light, truth, and guidance in our lives. He has saved me and He Himself is my salvation. He is my Savior. So whom shall I fear? Think about it. If God is the One who saves us, and we really believe that, we will not fear anyone. Remember, the Bible says that "Everyone who calls on the name of the Lord will be saved" (**Acts 2:21**). Anita and crew called on Jesus, and He saved them!

• •

Prayer Declaration – Lord, I, along with David declare by faith that "You are my light and my salvation. You are the strength and defense of my life. Whom shall I fear? Though people oppose me and attack me, I will not be afraid. And even if actual war arises around me, I am not shaken or moved. I love You, Lord, and by Your grace will stand firm in the face of life's battles.

Day 6

All My Fears

Psalm 34:4 – "I sought the LORD, and He answered me, And delivered me from all my fears.

You probably don't think of king David, the giant killer, as a man who had to deal with fear. According to Psalm 34, that idea about him is a myth. Although he was a man of valor and courage, he admits to having to deal with several fears as well. How do we reconcile such a seeming contradiction in David? Just because someone is a courageous hero doesn't mean that he never has to deal with fear. The fact is that everyone has to deal with fear in one way or another; some more than others. But the important point is that David learned how to be set free from his fears; how to be delivered from fear. And that's what we want to think about and learn today.

First, David says, "***all*** *my fears*." That tells us that there is no fear from which the Lord cannot deliver us. To say otherwise is to infer that God isn't stronger than fear. We must first admit that God can set free from any fear, no matter how debilitating it may seem to be at the moment. Then we'll be on the path of deliverance.

Claustrophobic types of fears used to often attack me and try to bring about panic in packed elevators, and other tight places. But like David, I sought the Lord and learned God's deliverance principles and was set free. Of course, as long as we are in this world we will experience different types of trials and tribulations because we have an adversary and demons to deal with. But even though fear or worry may try to attack, especially in certain situations, I know how to overcome. I live from a place of strength and victory. I also know how to do preemptive strikes against them before they can ambush me.

Lastly, notice the first phrase, "*I sought the Lord*." He got the answer and was delivered from fear while he was seeking the Lord. That is how I received the answers the Lord gave to me personally in different fearful situations. We should be seeking the Lord daily. He tells us to "seek and we will find" (**Matthew 7:7**). Ask and cry out to the Lord, and you will find that He will hear your call, and deliver you from all your fears.

• •

Prayer Declaration – Lord, I thank You that Your will is to deliver me from every single fear and worry. I am a seeker. I will seek You, and You will deliver me from all my fear. Hallelujah!

Day 7

Perfect Peace in Old Age

Psalm 37:25 – "I have been young and now I am old, Yet I have not seen the righteous forsaken Or his descendants begging bread."

Isaiah 46:4 - "Even to *your* old age I will be the same, And even to *your* graying years I will bear *you!* I have done *it*, and I will carry *you*; And I will bear *you* and I will deliver *you*."

Our first year of marriage, I was an exchange student in Mainz, Germany. During the winter break we traveled to Italy, and other countries as well. One day we went to a market to find some things to eat. A gypsy woman with a baby came up to me and held out her hand, begging for money. I didn't have much money myself but decided to give her a little anyway. After I walked away a few steps, I turned around just in time to see her pull a big bottle of wine out of her clothes and chug several big gulps. Well, I blew that money. But although I was young and naïve, God still blessed me for being generous.

I was twenty-five then. At the time of this writing, I am sixty. I may not be considered that old, but I'm not young like I used to be either. And in my short sixty years I've traveled and preached the gospel in many countries. In all these years, I've seen some poor Christians, but never any that were begging for bread. And although there have been times in my life when I didn't have much either, I've never had to beg for food. God has never forsaken my family or me.

There is no need for a Christian to fear or worry about old age. But to safeguard our heart, we must feed our mind on God's thoughts, promises, and truths. That is what builds faith. If we just look at what is happening to others, it could cause us to fear or worry. We must meditate on and believe God's promises concerning future years and old age.

David is saying that He has never seen the righteous, true believers, forsaken when they are old and possibly can't care for themselves. What does that mean to me? It means that the Lord won't ever abandon me. He will take care of me in old age just as He did when I was young! I will never go begging for bread! Hallelujah. He will feed and care for me more than He does for the birds of the air.

• •

Prayer Declaration – Lord, I thank You that You have made me righteous by the blood of Jesus. I also thank You that I will never have to beg for food. You are my good Heavenly Father, and You care for me. Even when I am old, You will care for me. Even in my graying years You will bear me, carry me, and deliver me. You will strengthen me and even when I die, my death will bring glory to You. Praise You, Lord!

Day 8

Uncommon Peace as the World Shakes

Psalm 46:1-3 – "God is our refuge and strength, A very present help in trouble.

2 Therefore we will not fear, though the earth should change And though the mountains slip into the heart of the sea;

3 Though its waters roar *and* foam, Though the mountains quake at its swelling pride."

One day I was on my balcony in Xi'an, China, and the strange thought came to my mind, "What would I do in the case of an earthquake?" I thought, "That's odd," and pondered for a few minutes what I might do and what I should do to prepare for such a calamity. Little did I realize it was the Holy Spirit revealing to me "things to come."

The next day, May 12, 2008, my family and I flew to Hong Kong. While we were still in the air, a powerful earthquake struck Wenchuan city and the surrounding area in Sichuan Province, China. The tremors mightily shook and even cracked buildings 500 kilometers away in Xi'an, our hometown.

Our friend Beverly was on the 13th floor of her apartment building when the earthquake struck. She said, "I was waiting for the elevator when the shaking began." There was a man standing beside her, waiting for the elevator as well. As the building shook, he became terrified. Beverly tried her best to comfort and assure him that it would be all right. She knew the Lord's protection, and also had experienced a few earthquakes before in Taiwan. So she was, at least to some degree, prepared for what was happening. She explained, "Then it began to shake more powerfully than I had ever felt before." Finally, after they had exited the building, and the shaking subsided, the man began to tell the others around him how astonished he was that Beverly had not panicked. She had an incredible peace. He could not comprehend how she was so calm during such a terrifying experience. This opened the door for Beverly to share with everyone around how she knew Jesus, and that He had given her the supernatural peace that passes understanding. God turned it into a mighty testimony for His glory.

Here in **Psalm 46**, it says that God is our refuge and strength. He is not just "a help," but a *very present* help in trouble. Sometimes we may think that He is a *far away*, very *distant* help to us in trouble. But that's what the devil wants you to think. And notice, David didn't say that there wouldn't be any trouble in our lives. He said that God would be a *very present help* in the troubles we encounter. When we begin to thank and praise Him for this, then our faith will undoubtedly grow.

Verse two then says, "Therefore we will not fear." Knowing verse one makes verse two possible in our lives. If we don't believe the truths about our Father God in verse one, then we'll be much more susceptible to fears. We need to speak these things out loud to ourselves. Speak them out by faith. That's what David did.

• •

Prayer Declaration – I thank You, Lord, that You are my refuge and strength. You aren't just present in my trouble. You are "very present." Praise You, Lord. Therefore I will not be afraid and am not afraid when calamities, tornadoes, earthquakes, and floods happen. You are my deliverer. You are my rescuer. You are my Lord and my God. You never leave me or forsake me. Even if the earth changes I won't be afraid because You never change and You are my God.

Day 9

Unshaken and Unmoved

Psalm 62:6 - "He only is my rock and my salvation, My stronghold; I shall not be shaken."

Isaiah 54:10 "For the mountains may be removed and the hills may shake, But My lovingkindness will not be removed from you, And My covenant of peace will not be shaken," Says the LORD who has compassion on you.

In the book of Exodus, when the judgments of God were coming upon the Egyptians, God's people in the district of Goshen were protected. The same protection was around Noah and his family when they obeyed the Lord, built the ark, and then went inside, surviving the worldwide flood of destruction. Judgments, floods, and famines have come to earth throughout the history of fallen man. And even though God's people saw the effects of these cataclysmic events, they were protected and preserved alive. We should expect and believe for the same. That doesn't mean you won't go through anything difficult. It means that God will protect you and provide for you.

"I shall not be shaken." The Psalmist makes a declaration here. When we have faith in God, we too will say so. We will declare it. We will say it out loud. We must release our faith for it to work for us. Here, David speaks out and then also writes out his positive confession/declaration of faith in God, His faithfulness, and provision.

If David were alive today and spoke this way, many would claim that he was a 'name-it-and-claim-it' faith preacher. But David knew his God and knew what faith in God could do. He had already seen it clearly in his battle with Goliath. David spoke some mighty bold words that day on the battlefield.

We likewise release worry and unbelief through words and deeds. Which are you going to speak? Faith in God, or faith in the devil? Unbelief toward God's Word, or unbelief in the doubts of the devil that try to fill your mind?

Finally, realize that God wants us to not just confidently say, "I know I'm saved and going to heaven." Praise God for that. But our faith in God and His promises should grow to the place where we also confidently say, "I will not be shaken" because we know God is our rock, our salvation, and our mighty stronghold.

• •

Prayer Declaration – God, I thank You that You are my rock, salvation, and stronghold. I have trusted in other things, but I am learning to trust more and more in You, and in You alone. And I thank You, Lord, that when I trust in You, I cannot be shaken, in Jesus' name! And even if mountains shake, Your love and kindness toward me will never shake or be removed from me. You have compassion toward me, and the covenant and promised peace of that covenant will not be shaken. You are helping me to grow in peace that cannot be shaken; that is firm and strong in You and Your promises.

Day 10

Peace Through Dwelling and Declaring

Psalm 91:1-2, 4 (NIV).

1 "Whoever dwells in the shelter of the Most High will rest in the shadow of the Almighty."

2 I will say of the Lord, "He is my refuge and my fortress, my God, in whom I trust."

4 "He will cover you with his feathers, and under his wings you will find refuge; his faithfulness will be your shield and rampart."

Myrtle Bailey was a Christian missionary in Hong Kong when the Japanese invaded in December of 1941. The Japanese had hung one of the missionaries just the day before, so fear was thick in the air around their school. The students were sent running home. The other missionaries had left weeks before this happened, so the young missionary woman was alone, thousands of miles from home.

The watchman pleaded, "Come with me! You can hide in my house until they leave. They'll kill you if they see you!"

She knew what the watchman said was true, but she could not accept leaving her little orphan girl, Faithy, behind. "Let's go now!" he demanded! When they arrived at the front gate of the compound, the old woman who washed clothes came running up to them and shrieked, "Faithy has just come in through the back gate!"

Myrtle ran back to the house. At that very moment, the Japanese soldiers came in through the front gate! It was too late. There was nowhere to go.

"Faithy! Where have you been?" Myrtle cried. "You run out the back gate as fast as you can go! Run to sister Water's house and stay quiet until I get there to take you with me."

Myrtle ran up the stairs of the mission house. No sooner had she entered her room than she heard soldier boots coming up the stairs. Tears were streaming down her face as she began to pray, "Oh Jesus, Jesus!"

Quickly they came down the hall and broke down the door where she was hiding. And then it happened! Feathers, lots and lots of feathers came raining down in the room and covered her body. She shivered and quaked inside until they covered her completely. The Japanese soldiers looked all around the room. They even looked directly at her, but could not see her! They slammed the door and continued their search through other rooms until they left the building.

Sister Bailey recognized that was a dramatic fulfillment of Psalm 91. "He shall cover you with His feathers, and under His wings shalt thou trust (Verse 4, KJV)." (Copyright 1995. Pete Snyder. *Let's Keep Moving*, pages 3-5. Engeltal Press)

Our God is a mighty God, and He will fulfill His Word, even Psalm 91, when we abide in His shadow and trust in Him.

• •

Prayer Declaration – Lord, I, like David, declare, "You are my refuge and fortress. My God, in whom I trust." You deliver me from traps of the enemy. You cover and protect me under your wings. I choose to dwell close to You, in Your shadow. No evil will happen to me or any plague come near my dwelling because I have made You, the Most High, my dwelling place.

Day 11

Ruling Peace

<u>Colossians 3:15</u> – "Let the peace of Christ rule in your hearts, to which indeed you were called in one body; and be thankful."

Did you know that certain parasites actually reprogram and control the minds of ants and snails? The ants and snails become like zombies, following the beck and call of the parasites. Mind control. It seems the whole world is trying to get control of our minds and influence our thoughts. This is exactly what the serpent (Satan) was trying to do with Eve in the beginning. And his strategy hasn't changed much through the years.

What most controls and influences your thinking? What kind of news and programming are you allowing and choosing to watch and listen to on the TV-Internet? They call what's on TV (and the Internet also) "programming." Right? What books do you read? What influences your beliefs in everyday life? God told us to "not be conformed to this world, but to be transformed by the renewing of our minds" with the Word of God (**Romans 12:2**).

You know, you can't have peace in the kingdom of your thought life when the world's lies and devil's propaganda (programming) are being broadcast freely in your mind every day. You have to turn them off and shut them up. Then you have to re-program your thought system with love, joy, righteousness, and peace programming that will build a stronghold of good thoughts, God's thoughts.

Jesus is the Prince of Peace, the King of Peace. When He is invited to come rule and reign in our hearts, peace will come. And when we actively seek out and meditate on His faith-inspiring and peace-giving words, then, more and more, worry and fear are driven out. Peace will be established.

Notice it says that *we* have to "let the peace rule." We have a part to play. Just because you are a Christian, doesn't mean that the peace and joy will go unchallenged. We have to enforce, by faith, the kingdom of peace. We have to choose each day to maintain God's peace in spite of stresses, problems, worries, and fears that are competing for control of our thoughts.

The word "rule" we see in verse 15 is similar to the authority that a referee or umpire has over sporting events such as baseball. The umpire calls the strikes and the outs. What he says goes. He "rules" and maintains order in the games. We also have to "make calls" and "rule" over the lies, worries, and fears that the devil will surely throw at us. Call the fearful thoughts the devil throws at you "balls," and let them go by. Recognize God's peaceful pitches. Swing at them, meditate on them, and you'll surely hit home runs in life!

• •

Prayer Declaration – Lord Jesus, I thank You that You are my Prince of Peace. Help me this day to grow, and learn to "let Your peace rule" in my heart. With Your help, I am the umpire of my thoughts. I run out the parasitic thoughts of fear and worry in Jesus' name. This day I will meditate on Your thoughts of peace, and let them rule in my heart. I will renew my mind, in Jesus' name!

Day 12

Believing He Is For Me

Psalm 118:6 – "The LORD is for me; I will not fear; what can man do to me?"

Knowing that our heavenly Father loves us and is for us is crucial to living a victorious Christian life. If the truth be told, many of us don't much feel the Lord is for us. Many Christians feel that the Lord really isn't too pleased or happy with them. But when we have truly repented of sin, and know that the Lord has forgiven us, we need to add to that the revelation that God really is for us. He loves you and sincerely is for you.

Of course, many Christians struggle with this because they compare themselves with others. Sometimes we see what others have and think, "God is for them. This verse is true for them." We struggle to believe that He is for us.

Think about the story of Joseph in the book of Genesis (**Genesis 37-50**). The Bible declares over and over that God's favor was on Joseph and that God was with Joseph. But Joseph might have struggled with believing that because for thirteen years he was in slavery. So just because you are in difficult circumstances doesn't necessarily mean that God isn't for you. If Joseph believed those thoughts, he would have been very mistaken. He would have been listening to the lies of the devil. Actually, God was not only for Joseph, but He loved and was for Joseph's brothers too.

He wanted them *all* to be blessed and succeed in life. God wasn't for their sin, of course. He wasn't for the way they mistreated Joseph. But He wanted them to admit they were wrong, be reconciled to their brother, and grow to be the men that He had destined for them to be. So wherever you are in that story, God is for you too. He wants to bless you more than you know.

So first of all, we need to meditate on this verse until the truth that He loves us and is for us begins to root itself deep into our spirits and mental DNA. When this starts to happen, the measure of fear in our lives related to not believing that God is really for us will begin to diminish and die. You see, when we don't believe that God is for us, we have a nagging feeling that we aren't pleasing to God, and so His promises won't work for us. Or we may feel that God couldn't be for me because "I've messed up so much in my life," or "I'm a weak Christian." But that is all a lie of the devil. When we confess and repent of the wrong we have done, God immediately forgives and restores relationship with us.

Then we need to begin to agree with God and declare, like the Psalmist, that He is for me. Our words are powerful and have tremendous influence in our lives. Research shows that most of us have very negative self-talk going on in our minds. So we must learn to counteract this by beginning to speak the truth of God's Word to ourselves.

• •

Prayer Declaration - God is for me. He is for my life to go well, and to have success. He wants me to win at walking in love and overcoming fear and worry in my life. I will not fear. If God is for me, what can man do to me?

Day 13

Setting Your Mind On The Spirit

Romans 8:6 – "For the mind set on the flesh is death, but the mind set on the Spirit is life and peace."

Arctic wolves normally are no match for musk oxen and bison. As long as the musk oxen stand their ground in their defensive perimeter, there is nothing that the wolves can do. It is only when the musk oxen give in to fearful emotions or panic and begin to run that the wolves can exploit the situation to their advantage. It is only when the musk oxen are fleeing that the wolves have a chance to steal, kill and destroy like **John 10:10** describes.

And so it is in our lives as well. If we give in to fearful thoughts and bolt in fear, then our fears will control and consume us. But if we learn to face our fears, stand our ground, and even run the wolves off, then we are becoming the overcomers we were called to be. Proverbs says, "The wicked flee when no one is pursuing but the righteous are as bold as a lion" (**Proverbs 28:1**). Faith in God and His promises, energized by the Holy Spirit, will help us to stand firm and see the wolves and lions run from us.

Romans 8:6 tells us that to have "life and peace" you must set your mind on the things that the Holy Spirit guides you to think on. The musk oxen sometimes do not keep their minds at peace. At times, they don't maintain their defensive and offensive strategies to defeat fear and arctic wolves. And so it is if we don't follow the divinely inspired strategies that Jesus has given to us in the Word of God. Remember, He is the One who inspired the writing of the Bible in the first place. So setting your mind on the Spirit is synonymous with setting your mind on the truth of God's Word.

In the NIV it describes the "flesh" as our "sinful nature." We aren't to allow sinful thoughts, emotions or desires that come to our mind to lead us or control us. Fear, worry, and panic are emotions that the devil will try to inspire or exploit to the fullest. It should be obvious to us that giving in to wrong thoughts is going to lead to trouble, and heartache. So learn to listen to the Holy Spirit, your Helper, and He will guide you into peace and a joyful life.

Pray, and ask the Lord to help you to "set your mind on the Spirit" today. Meditate on the Word of God, and listen in your spirit.

• •

Prayer Declaration – Lord, thank You that through the help of the Holy Spirit I can control my mind and my thoughts. I can decide what to set my mind and thoughts on. Today I choose to agree with the Holy Spirit and set my mind on life and peace. I will not allow my mind to be "set" on fear, worry, anger, or lust. I will think God's thoughts and speak God's thoughts of life and peace today, in Jesus' name!

Day 14

Protection From All Evil

Psalm 121:7,8 – "The LORD will protect you from all evil; He will keep your soul.

8 The LORD will guard your going out and your coming in from this time forth and forever."

Anita and I took a youth team from our church (Reserve Church, now Lifehouse Church) to protest and sidewalk counsel in front of the Delta Abortion mill on St. Charles Avenue, New Orleans, LA. It was about 1985, and our church always had teams going on Saturday mornings to try to save unborn babies and help their mothers. Anita and I didn't have much experience, and no training at all, but we had a deep conviction from God that what we were doing was right and God's will.

That day there were about 10 or 12 young people who went on the outreach with us. We had signs and were walking in a circle on the sidewalk in front of the entrance of the building. People had to walk past us to get to the doors. We had been there for twenty or thirty minutes when I saw a guy I recognized coming our way. He had come close to physically attacking one of our team members in an adult group the month before. So when I saw him, I immediately warned everyone in the group to keep their mouths shut and not give him an excuse to bother us.

Well, that day he didn't need any excuse. I think that he actually was sent by the abortion mill workers to do what he did. Be that as it may, he got about halfway past our team and then began to attack one of the young guys verbally. He got in his face and forced him over against the wall of the abortion mill. He was railing on the brother, so I quickly walked over and stood beside him to distract him. He then turned to me and started shouting and pushing. I knelt down on the sidewalk and started praying out loud for him. He tried to kick me and knock me over. Finally, he pulled some tracts out that I had in my back pocket, tore them up, and walked off mumbling to himself. I settled our group, and we called the police to report what had happened.

Why do I share this story? God protected us in what could have turned into a violent encounter. And the Holy Spirit was able to diffuse the situation because we responded in the right Spirit. Jesus said that we would be persecuted when we sought to live godly lives (**1 Tim. 3:12**). So persecution is to be expected. But God said that He would "protect us from all evil," and He certainly did that day.

When we are humbly and closely following the Lord, we can claim these verses by faith, and enjoy the peace that comes from believing that He will indeed protect us from all evil.

• •

Prayer Declaration – Lord, I thank You for your promises of protection. I thank You that You will keep me from all evil. You will protect me today when I go out, and when I return. I claim Your protection as I drive, fly and travel. I am not afraid because you are my strength and shield.

Day 15

Put Your Trust In God

Psalm 56:3 When I am afraid, I will put my trust in You.

4 In God, whose word I praise, In God I have put my trust; I shall not be afraid.

Psalm 107:6 Then they cried out to the LORD in their trouble; He delivered them out of their distresses.

In 1990 I was the director/pastor of a missionary boot camp and language school called Calvary Ministerial Language School in El Carmen, Mexico, just outside of Monterrey. It is a branch of Calvary Ministerial Institute. We had groups of missionary candidates that would come each year for training and language learning. That year, three of the students (Paul Brill, Jeff Salard and Phil Long) and myself decided to climb El Fraile (the Friar), the mountain facing the school on the other side of the river. It had a gradual slope, so I figured it wouldn't be too difficult to climb, and we should be able to do it in a day. We got up early one Saturday and drove to the base of the mountain.

I should have known that there would be problems from the beginning because the two single guys didn't eat any breakfast that morning and didn't bring any water with them either! It was extremely hot and dry at that time of the year in northern Mexico as temperatures soared way above 100 degrees. Each one of us had needed to bring plenty of water for the climb. So actually we were set up for failure from the beginning. But we pressed on ahead anyway and thought we'd just share the water we had between us.

We climbed the cactus-covered mountain for a few hours, and as you might imagine, I noticed that our water supply was going fast. I told the guys we'd have to ration what we had left. After a couple more hours I finally saw a ridge that might be the top. I thought we could make it there and then we'd have reached the summit. So we pressed on further. But when we took the last few steps over the ridge our hearts sank as we saw that it was a false summit. The top was still at least two or three hours of climbing away. Our water was almost gone, and we were already pretty dehydrated when I told them that there was no way we could make it safely to the top that day. We had to turn back.

As we admitted defeat and headed back down, I realized that our bodies had stopped sweating. We were already dehydrated. My three companions, sensing the dangerous predicament we were in, and looking for any way to get down quicker, saw a ravine and felt we'd move much faster that way. I warned them that it would likely have more undergrowth, and make the going more difficult. Moreover, there was no guarantee we'd be able to make it down that way. But they wanted to try it anyway, so I finally agreed.

It didn't take long until we reached an impassable spot. We couldn't go any further. We were stuck on the mountainside. I told the guys we'd have to go back up to where we began descending. It was too dangerous to risk going any further that way. So with our limited amount of strength, we had to climb back up to where we started, and then go down from there on our original path.

When we made it back, we were exhausted. We rationed out the last few swallows of water, drank it all, and headed down. We could see the truck, loaded with an ice chest of refreshing, cold water, at the base of the mountain, seemingly mocking us, several hours of painful descent off in the distance.

At one point we took a break and crawled under a bush to try to find some limited shade to protect us from the scorching sun. I could see that Jeff's lips were cracked. He was severely dehydrated. At that point, I was concerned even more about whether or not all of us would actually make it down okay. I began to pray and cry out to the Lord (**Ps.107:6**), "God have mercy on our foolishness, and help us all to make it down safely."

Finally, Phil said, "Guys, we need to get moving." So we wearily raised ourselves to our feet and started working our way down around the cactus and thorn bushes that covered the mountain.

The sky was pure blue the whole day, without even a wisp of a cloud to block the blazing sun. On any other day, it would have been beautiful. But that day, and at that point, it seemed cruel and unforgiving.

As we stumbled down the mountain, at one point I glanced up and was amazed to see a tiny, dense, dark, black cloud, the size of a man's fist, reminding me of the kind of cloud that Elijah must have seen after the three years of drought (**1 Kings 18:44**).

I watched the cloud as it astonishingly moved straight toward us! We gazed in wonder, amazement, and thanksgiving as that tiny, single cloud came right over us and began to soak us with cool, refreshing rain! God had heard our cry! We spread out our neckerchiefs to soak up the rain and opened our mouths to catch as many raindrops as we could. Through that incredible act of God's mercy, we were able to find enough rainwater on the leaves and in the rock crevasses to drink and therefore make it down the mountain, and back to the truck where more water was waiting for us. Praise God.

"They were hungry and thirsty; Their soul fainted within them. Then they cried out to the LORD in their trouble; He delivered them out of their distresses" (**Psalm 107:5,6**).

What do you do when you are afraid? David declared, "I put my trust in God," and His praiseworthy Word.

• •

Prayer Declaration - I trust in You, Lord. And I will not be afraid. You are with me and will help me. I will lighten the load on my heart by speaking Your 'good words.' I cry to You when I am in trouble, and You hear me and rescue me. Thank You, Lord. I trust in You. Hallelujah!

Day 16

That It May Go Well With Your Children

Proverbs 1:33 - "But he who listens to me shall live securely And will be at ease from the dread of evil."

Deuteronomy 4:40 "So you shall keep His statutes and His commandments which I am giving you today, that it may go well with you and with your children after you."

In 1991, we were missionaries in El Carmen, Mexico. One day my wife, Anita, came to me distraught and said she couldn't find Esther, our six-year-old daughter, anywhere. Her older sister, Lydia, didn't know where she was either. So we began to look for her and call for her everywhere. No one knew where she was. We looked and asked people at the Bible School where we worked. We looked all over the school property where we lived, which was around 15 acres or so. Everybody was looking for her. Nothing. I went to a well the students were digging near where we lived. There wasn't any protective barricade around it, so I looked there to see if she had fallen in. We looked for what seemed like 30 minutes to an hour. Desperation was rising and we were calling on the Lord to help us.

Your un-renewed mind, along with the devil, will bring every worst-case scenario to your thoughts, and tell you that you will never see your daughter again. We were battling those fearful thoughts, doing our best to trust in the Lord in the midst of a parent's worst nightmare.

Finally, after what seemed like an eternity, we found her right under our noses. All that time she had been next door in a little neighbor girl's house where Anita had actually asked before, but they responded, "No. She's not here." For some reason we came back later and asked a second time. This time a different person came to the door and said, "Yes, sure. She's here playing with our daughter." We both breathed out a collective sigh of massive relief!

We determined that while Anita was washing clothes, Esther had crawled through our back fence to play with the little neighbor girl. She had never played at her house before. But even though we didn't know where she was, God was protecting and watching over her all the time.

Without the Lord to rely on in such situations, it would be easy to go crazy with fear and grief. Thankfully, since that time we have learned to listen to the Lord, allow Him to calm our fears, and put faith and trust where once was worry and panic. The Lord loves our children more than we do.

At times my wife would be concerned about our own children and we would pray for them. I always told her, "We need to say, 'Our kids are going to turn out right. They are going to love and serve the Lord. They are going to fulfill God's will for their lives, in Jesus' name.'" And thank God, all of our children love God, serve the Lord in the local church, and want to fulfill His will for their lives. We spoke our faith, released it, and it worked in our kids. It will work for yours too.

Take control of your thoughts, and tune in to God's radio station, W-P-E-A-C-E, peace. Allow His top ten songs and melodies to flow through your mind, wash out the trash, and deposit faith.

• •

Prayer Declaration – Lord, I thank You for Your precious promises. I thank You that when I listen and pay attention to Your words, I have Your supernatural security and peace. I thank You that my children will love and serve You all the days of their lives. Thank You, Lord, in Jesus' name.

Day 17

Sweet Sleep

Proverbs 3:13, 17, 24 - "How blessed is the man who finds wisdom."

17 "Her ways are pleasant ways And all her paths are peace."

24 "When you lie down, you will not be afraid; When you lie down, your sleep will be sweet."

As I've lived in different countries, I've seen people sleeping outside on hard tables, and on the bare ground. Once I even saw a man sleeping balanced on a thick chain, draped and hung between two poles like a hammock! I saw another man in Cambodia sleeping in a hammock that he had tied up inside of the cart on the back of his motorcycle taxi. I've seen little children sleeping on bicycles while their parents pedaled them on the way home. I've often thought how amazing it is that some people can sleep almost anywhere and at any time. Many of these people were poor people without much money in life, and yet they seemed to be sleeping without a care or worry. Would you like to be able to fall asleep and sleep a deep, peaceful sleep like that? Here in Proverbs, He tells us how.

Fear is obviously something that can hinder and rob us of peace and sleep. Here in **Proverbs 3**, King Solomon, who at one time was one of the wisest men, if not the wisest man to ever be a king, gives Holy-Spirit-anointed wisdom for being blessed, walking in peace, and being able to lie down to sweet sleep.

The first key that he gives is to find God's kind of wisdom. That means you have to search for it. God is the source of wisdom and therefore asking Him for wisdom, and seeking it in the Bible, are crucial elements to finding the wisdom you need that will bring supernatural peace to your life.

Verse 17 says that you have to "take hold of her," and also "hold her fast (tightly)." You have to obey the wisdom, and then also be diligent to keep doing what it says. Why? Because if you don't hold onto it, and hold it tightly, you will most likely lose it.

Verse 24 says, "when you lie down, you will not be afraid....Your sleep will be sweet." People spend a lot of money and take a lot of medicines trying to get a good night's sleep. Here God tells us that if we follow His Word and Wisdom, we can keep our money, not have to take sleep medications, and then sleep sweetly, free from worry and fear.

• •

Prayer Declaration – Lord, I thank You because I am blessed. I am blessed by the wisdom and understanding You are giving me. When I heed Your wisdom, I will walk in peace and happiness.

When I lie down I can fall asleep peacefully, with no nagging worries, fear of a break-in or attack. My sleep will be sweet in Jesus' name. Tonight I will sleep like a baby, in Jesus' name.

Day 18

God Planned For Your Peace

Jeremiah 29:11 - "'For I know the plans that I have for you,' declares the LORD, 'plans for welfare [good, well-being, to prosper] and not for calamity to give you a future and a hope.'"

Many people in the world today, including some Christians, are apprehensive and fearful about their futures. Others are afraid for the future of their marriages, the future of their children and families, the future of their jobs, their countries, churches, businesses, and many things. Some Christians are afraid of what the Bible calls "the great tribulation" (**Matthew 24**), being persecuted for Jesus, or rejected because of their faith. We live in a tumultuous world, and things are shaking that we thought were rock solid. This is why it is so important to be living in the will of God. The only place where you can be sure of God's protection and watch care is knowing and walking in the will and plan of God for your life.

My father and mother-in-law were missionaries in Brazil for over 40 years. Some people criticized them for "taking their children off to a third world country (This was back in the late 40's, 50's and 60's in Brazil)." My wife and I have also been criticized and questioned for taking our children off to Russia and China, "dangerous places." But I, like my father-in-law, would respond by saying, "The safest place for anyone to be is in the will of God, whatever country or neighborhood that may be."

But the amazing thing is that many people, many Christians even, are afraid of God's will. They don't understand God, Who He is, and how much He loves them. For those who love God, look at what He said to us through Jeremiah the prophet in the verse above. First of all, He confirms that He has plans for you! God created you and planned a great life for you. Easy? No. Fulfilling? Yes.

What is His plan for us like? His plan is for our welfare, benefit, prosperity, and good. Isn't that what God planned and did for Abraham, as well as for the children of Israel in their Promised Land? Sure it was. And the Bible says that we have a better covenant than they had!

He also says that He wants to give you hope for a good and better future. Doesn't that remind you of what Jesus said? "I have come to give you life, and life more abundant" (**John 10:10**). God's plan is for us to have abundant life filled with love, joy, peace, and prosperity. His plan is for us to have abundant supernatural power to bless the world and bring God abundant glory.

Don't allow the devil to make you afraid of the future. If you love God and are seeking to follow Him, He says that He "will fulfill His purpose" for your life (**Psalm 138:8**).

• •

Prayer Declaration – Lord, I thank You that You will fulfill Your purpose for me. I thank You that You have a good and awesome plan for my life. Your plan is for my good. I thank You that in Christ I have a good future. Hallelujah!

Day 19

Peace In The Storm

Isaiah 41:10 - "Do not fear, for I am with you; Do not anxiously look about you, for I am your God. I will strengthen you, surely I will help you, Surely I will uphold you with My righteous right hand."

December 31, 1932, Bertha Smith, missionary to China, was on a ship bound for the Orient. In spite of her mission board informing her that they could not provide her with financial support because of the Great Depression, she returned to China anyway, knowing the call of God, and that He, not a mission board, was her source.

She and another travelling companion had been witnessing to the others on the ship without much success. But then the worse storm the ship's crew had ever seen fell upon them. About noon a part of a tremendous wave struck the ship. Dishes, silverware, and food went smashing in every direction. Men turned white with fear, and women screamed as they were hurled across the lounge. No sooner was one such shock over than a similar one followed.

The first officer had the responsibility of the passengers. He looked like death itself as he moved around giving tranquilizers to the people. Sister Bertha and her traveling companion didn't need any. Everyone could see that their expressions were testimonies of peace and calm.

One young Russian lady named Lyuba was begging for someone to pray. The Jews sat helplessly around her, unable to pray or comfort. Sister Bertha went to her and began to pray. She told her with calm assurance that they would arrive in Shanghai safely. She told her that Jesus Himself had come aboard the ship in Los Angeles when Bertha got on, since He was living in her heart. The ship would not go down! She read to her passages of peace from God's Word and sang to her several hymns. Later that afternoon, Lyuba prayed to receive Jesus as her Lord and Savior. A greater storm in her heart than the one against the ship had been raging for her soul.

Soon the seas calmed and they sailed the remainder of the journey under smiling skies. The first officer admitted only to Miss Huey and Sister Bertha that he had expected the whole deck floor to blow off, which would have meant the death of them all. ("Go Home and Tell." Pages 44-46. Bertha Smith. Broadman Press)

Our Scripture for today was fulfilled in Sister Bertha and Miss Huey. They did "not fear" because they knew the promise that God was "with them." We can readily see how important it is for us to have an unshakable, rock-solid faith that <u>God is with us</u>. It needs to be part of the bedrock of our faith and relationship with God, our Father. So again, meditate on this verse and others that affirm that fact that God is with you. Tell yourself, like King David did, that God is with you. Feed your faith and starve your doubts.

• •

<u>Prayer Declaration</u> – Lord, I thank You that You are with me, and therefore I do not and will not fear, in Jesus' name. I will not anxiously look around me because You are my God, and You will meet my needs. I don't need to look for

any other god. I thank You that You will help me and uphold me throughout my life. I rejoice and praise You for
setting me free from fear and worry for You are my Provider.

Day 20

Perfect Peace

Isaiah 26:3 (KJV) - "Thou wilt keep *him* in perfect peace, *whose* mind *is* stayed *on thee:* because he trusteth in thee."

On Monday, November 19, 2007, 92-year-old Pauline "Polly" Jacobi had placed her groceries on the driver's side back seat of her car, which was parked in one of the spots for disabled people near the grocery side entrance of the Wal-Mart Super Center in Dyersburg, Tennessee. She got into the car and was about to start the engine when the front passenger door suddenly opened, and an unkempt looking man jumped in!

"Give me your money!" He said to her. She said, "No, you're not getting my money." Twice more the desperate man demanded her money. The third time he said that if she didn't give him her money, he would kill her.

"Then the Lord took over," Pauline said. She told him, "If you kill me, I'm going straight to heaven, but you're going to hell. Jesus is in this car, and He goes with me wherever I go!" The man just stared at her in disbelief!

"You look like you've had an awful time in this world," she said to him. "And as bad as that is, it's nothing compared to hell."

She looked intently at the man's eyes as she talked with him. "He had such sad eyes," she said.

"I asked him his name. He said it was Ricky."

"Ricky, you drink, don't you?" asked Pauline. "He said he was hungry. I said if you didn't spend your money on drink you'd have money for a meal."

"Then I asked him, 'Ricky, would you like to go to heaven?'"

"Yes, I sure would," he said. "But I'm afraid the Lord won't take me."

"Yes, he will. He will take you if you believe. He'd save you right here and now. All you have to do is believe in Him and accept Him as your Savior." He told her, "I think I'll go home tonight and pray." "Oh, you can pray anytime you want, " she said. "Anytime, anywhere."

Pauline reached into her purse and took out all the money she had, $10. She told Ricky she was giving him her money. "Don't spend it on whiskey! Get something to eat!" she said to him.

He hesitated. "I want you to have it," she said. "You weren't going to take it from me, but I will give it to you."

He looked away from her as tears began to fill his eyes. Then the tears started to stream down his face. She talked with him for over 10 minutes. Then he leaned over and kissed her on the cheek. He was shaken by the encounter he had just had. He opened the door and walked off into the night.

Ninety-two-year-old Pauline Jacobi had perfect peace even in the midst of an attempted robbery. How could she respond with such courage and confidence during such a terrifying situation? That's what we want to look at today. (http://www.stategazette.com/story/1294862.html)

Perfect peace and a steadfast, right-thinking mind go hand in hand. Pauline had been filling her mind with God's thoughts for the 70 years that she had been a church member. It was natural for her to respond the way she did. And it can be for you too. Get to know Him better today.

• •

Prayer Declaration – Lord, I thank You that I can discipline and control my thoughts. I do discipline my mind to think about Jesus, His life, and His promises. I thank You, Lord, that I can have perfect peace in my heart and mind.

Day 21

Jesus Left Us Special Peace

John 14:27 - "Peace I leave with you; My peace I give to you; not as the world gives do I give to you. Do not let your heart be troubled, nor let it be fearful.

On October 15, 1932, Gladys Aylward travelled by train to China to be a missionary. She travelled by train because she didn't have enough money for ship passage. But she knew that God had called her, and she went even though no mission agency would support her. After a harrowing journey through Russia and northeast China, she finally made it to Yangcheng. She went to help veteran, widowed, independent, Scottish missionary Jeannie Lawson, who with her outreach through an inn would preach to the mule train drivers that regularly came through their town. But after a short time sister Jeannie died from injuries she suffered in a fall. Gladys was left all alone. She didn't know what she would do since she had no way to sustain the work of the inn. But she knew that the same God who had brought her safely to China had left His peace with her. She called out to Him in prayer and trusted Him to meet her needs. Did she feel peaceful? Probably not. But she was not controlled by her feelings. She took hold of the promise of God anyway, and did "not let her heart be troubled or fearful."

Not long after, the local Mandarin (magistrate) came to visit her and asked her to consider taking a position in his local government. A new law against women's foot binding had been passed, and they needed a foot inspector. Gladys seemed to be the perfect choice to go from village to village, checking women's feet to make sure the law was enforced. This way, God not only supplied her financial needs, but also opened the door for her to preach the gospel in all the villages in her surrounding area.

When Jesus left the earth, He left His peace with all true believers. He says that it is His special peace, "My peace." It's the same peace that resides inside of Him! That is an unshakable, unmovable, supernatural, beyond-comprehension peace. The world can't give this kind of peace. The world gives peace if things are peaceful, and your bank account is full, your savings account is full, or you have whatever it is that you feel you have to have in order to feel secure. But Jesus tells us, "Believe that you have my peace. *You* take control of your situation and don't let your heart be troubled. *You* don't let fear grip you." It's not a suggestion. Jesus wants us to grow up, and therefore tells us that the responsibility is ours. If we want to walk in peace, we will have to appropriate His grace and peace by faith.

• •

Prayer Declaration – Lord, I thank You today that You left supernatural peace, Your peace, with me. It's a peace that the world cannot give. You are the source and Prince of Peace, and You live in me! I don't let my heart be fearful or troubled. I praise You that You are with me. I stay in Your presence and Your courts with worship, thanksgiving and praise on my lips. Hallelujah.

Day 22

Peace Through Knowing The Father

Matthew 6:25,26,33,34 - "For this reason I say to you, do not be worried about your life, as to what you will eat or what you will drink; nor for your body, as to what you will put on. Is not life more than food, and the body more than clothing?

26 "Look at the birds of the air, that they do not sow, nor reap nor gather into barns, and yet your heavenly Father feeds them. Are you not worth much more than they?

33 "But seek first His kingdom and His righteousness, and all these things will be added to you.

34 "So do not worry about tomorrow; for tomorrow will care for itself. Each day has enough trouble of its own."

You may not be aware, but no other religion in the world has a god that says he is a **father** to us. Praise God, we have a loving heavenly Father who not only is Almighty God of the Universe but also our Father who cares for us, loves us, and supernaturally meets our needs.

Building these verses into our hearts will push back at the pressures of anxiety and fear that come against us all. You have seen the experiment when a metal can is heated, and therefore the air inside the can becomes warmer than the air outside. Then it is sealed. As time passes, the air inside the can cools, and as it does the can begins to implode and crinkle as it is crushed under the normal atmospheric pressure around it. The can was fine as long as the pressure inside pushing out was the same as the pressure outside the can pushing in. But when a partial vacuum was formed on the inside, by the change in air molecules and pressure, the can soon began to slowly implode by the greater air pressure on the outside. Likewise, if we don't fill our spirits and minds with God's truths as we see here in **Matthew 6:11-34**, we won't have enough power in us to push out against the thoughts of worry, fear, and anxiety that try to bombard us every day. We have to fill our hearts with God's thoughts.

Matthew 6:33 is like a powerful, peace-filled spiritual sedative. We don't need a glass of wine or sedatives to relax. God and His Word are our peace.

• •

Prayer Declaration – Lord, I thank You, that You are a good Father. You daily meet my needs, physical and spiritual. I don't worry about what I'm going to eat, drink, or wear. I don't worry about where I'm going to live, or work. You are Jehovah Jireh, my Provider. You take care of the birds and flowers. How much more will You take care of me? I don't worry about tomorrow because You hold the future in Your hands, and You love me.

Day 23

Peace Over Sudden Fear

<u>Hebrews 13:5, 6</u> - "…for He Himself has said, "I WILL NEVER DESERT YOU, NOR WILL I EVER FORSAKE YOU,"

6 so that we confidently say, "THE LORD IS MY HELPER, I WILL NOT BE AFRAID. WHAT WILL MAN DO TO ME?"

<u>Proverbs 3:25</u> – "Do not be afraid of sudden fear…"

It was the summer of 1986 and my wife, and I were interim pastors at Ashland Christian Fellowship, a little mission church in Ashland, Montana on the edge of the Northern Cheyenne Native American Reservation. Mitch Pousson had helped us during that summer, but now was the time for him to return home to Louisiana. We drove to Billings and were staying in a Motel Six that night to be ready to get him to the airport early the next morning.

We got adjacent rooms with a door in between. Mitch was in one room by himself, and my wife and I, along with our two little girls, were in the other room. We were sleeping soundly when suddenly, banging and screaming shocked me awake! Someone was beating on our door, angrily yelling for us to "open up and let him in!" I bolted out of bed, ran to the door and pulled back the window curtain to see a wild-eyed man staring back at me. I shouted, "What are you doing?!" Startled and aggravated, he realized he was at the wrong place and marched off down the outdoor walkway. I didn't have a gun, so brandishing a weapon wasn't an option. Of course, in the midst of the man screaming and me shouting at him, my wife was wide-awake, and now trying to comfort our crying girls.

I was upset how he had frightened us and caused my girls to wake up crying. We tried our best to settle back down and get back to sleep. The problem was there was no phone in the room to call the police or the front desk. To save money and make their motel more economical, Motel Six had no phones in their rooms in those days. Tom Bodett would "keep the light on" but not provide a telephone.

Then, after about five or ten minutes had passed and we were settling down, there was a knock on the door in between our rooms. What now? I went to the door and quietly asked, "Who is this?" Of course, it was Mitch, but I wasn't taking any chances after what had just happened. I laugh about it now, but it wasn't too funny that night.

He said, "It's me, Mitch. Someone was banging on my door trying to get in." I opened the door between our rooms and told him the same thing happened to us. I said, "It's okay. Go back to sleep. Even though I think he's on drugs, I believe he knows he had the wrong room and we won't be seeing him again."

We all went back to sleep and rested peacefully the rest of the night. I thank God that in scary situations we always have a heavenly telephone number we can dial up by faith, **Hebrews 13: 6** or **Proverbs 3:25, 26** on the Bible hotline. The pre-recorded message we'll hear is there to comfort us, build up our faith, and affirm to us that God will never desert us or forsake us.

• •

Prayer Declaration - Lord, I thank You that although others may desert me, You will never desert me or forsake me. You are my Helper. I am not afraid of sudden fear, in Jesus' name. I won't be afraid of the wicked because You are my confidence. Praise God!

Day 24

Only Believe

Luke 8:50 – "But when Jesus heard *this,* He answered him, 'Do not be afraid *any longer;* only believe...'"

Act 27:25 "Therefore, keep up your courage, men, for I believe God that it will turn out exactly as I have been told."

"Do not be afraid, only believe." Faith in God is what will make the difference. What is the only thing, according to this verse, we should be doing? "Only believe."

Paul and his traveling companions were on their way to Rome (**Acts 27**), where Paul would have to stand trial before Caesar. Paul sensed in his spirit that calamity was coming to their voyage if they didn't stay and harbor for winter where they were. He warned the captain and the pilot, but they didn't listen to him. As a result, after they weighed anchor and headed out to sea their ship was suddenly caught in a powerful typhoon. How many storms in life we could have avoided if we had just learned to listen to the warnings of the Holy Spirit, and godly counsel around us.

They fasted for two weeks, and most the men gave up hope and thought they wouldn't make it through the storm alive. But at this critical moment Paul stood up and told the men, "Men, you ought to have followed my advice and not to have set sail from Crete and incurred this damage and loss.

"Yet now I urge you to keep up your courage, for there will be no loss of life among you, but only of the ship.

"For this very night an angel of the God to whom I belong and whom I serve stood before me, saying, 'Do not be afraid, Paul; you must stand before Caesar; and behold, God has granted you all those who are sailing with you.' "Therefore, keep up your courage, men, for I believe God that it will turn out exactly as I have been told" (**Acts 27:22-25**). That last phrase is a powerful declaration of faith that I have used many times in my life, believing for healing, praying for my children, finances, or other prayer requests. "I believe God that it will turn out exactly as I have been told" in the Word of God, or by the Spirit of God. And praise God, it did turn out just exactly as Paul had been told. Was it easy? No. They still suffered shipwreck and had to swim to shore, but at least they were all alive.

We all must grow to the place where Paul was, and say with confidence along with him, "I believe God that it will turn out exactly as I was told," as the Word of God says. Receive God's peace. "Do not be afraid any longer. Only believe."

• •

Prayer Declaration – Lord, I thank You that I can hear Your voice through the pages of Scripture, and I'm not "afraid any longer. I only believe that it will turn out just as Your Word says."

Day 25

Don't Fear the Heat

<u>Jeremiah 17:7, 8 (Daniel 3:14-28)</u> - "Blessed is the man who trusts in the LORD And whose trust **is** the LORD.

8 "For he will be like a tree planted by the water, That extends its roots by a stream And **<u>will not fear when the heat comes</u>**; But its leaves will be green, And it will not be anxious in a year of drought Nor cease to yield fruit.

Spiritual people don't walk by feelings, or by the way things appear. We are to walk by faith, trusting in the Lord and His promises. If you are ruled and guided by your emotions and feelings, along with what you see and hear in the news every day, you will be a defeated, depressed Christian.

Does that mean that problems, troubles and fiery furnace heat won't come to us at times? No. God never said that we wouldn't have any problems in life. In fact, He says that we will experience trials and tests. But our destiny is to walk in the fire and not be burned! God's will for us is to "not fear when the heat comes," when the trials and tests come.

Hananiah, Mishael, and Azariah, otherwise known as Shadrach, Meshach, and Abed-nego, were tested by *the heat* very severely. In fact, in **Daniel chapter three** they were commanded to bow down before the king's idol.

But they were worshippers of the One True God and therefore flatly refused. As a result, the king threatened them with Babylonian capital punishment, which was to be thrown into a "fiery furnace." It's interesting that the furnace was called "fiery." You'd think that would be obvious, but the Babylonians wanted to make sure people got the message!

But what the king didn't know was that Daniel's friends, Hananiah, Mishael and Azariah, had a faith that was fierier than the furnace. And do you know what their fiery faith did for them? It gave them courage, moreover, courage to such a degree that they were not afraid of that furnace, or death by being burned alive. We might say they didn't "fear the heat" when it came! How can that be? Well, part of the answer is that they were men who feared God. But more importantly, God was in the fire with them, and He is in your fire with you!

• •

Prayer Declaration – Lord, I thank You, that I can control my thoughts and emotions. I don't let my heart "be troubled." And by Your grace, I don't fear "when the heat comes." I'm not anxious about economic downturns or if I lose my job. My job is not my source, You are. You are my loving heavenly Father, and I have a secret economy that cares for me and meets my every need, in Jesus' name. Thank You, Lord.

Day 26

Weapons To Fight For Peace

2 Corinthians 10:4,5 "for the weapons of our warfare are not of the flesh, but divinely powerful for the destruction of fortresses.

5 *We are* destroying speculations (imaginations) and every lofty thing raised up against the knowledge of God, and *we are* taking every thought captive to the obedience of Christ."

My brother was a "crop duster" AG pilot. He flew airplanes, fertilizing and spraying chemicals over fields in the Mississippi Delta. Over the course of his career, he had several crashes and emergency landings. His co-worker pilots had similar experiences, although I don't think any of them had quite as many close calls and brushes with death like my brother. My parents, his wife, my sister and I often prayed for God's protection over him.

I remember my brother telling me about one of the other pilots who had also had a crash landing. He had recovered and was now going to start flying again. My brother said, "He (my friend) went up for a short test flight to get back into flying. He soon finished his practice run, but when he got out of the plane he was soaking wet with sweat, and looked completely worn out." Why? He had to fight the fear of getting back into that airplane and flying again. It's not easy to do that when you've had a life-threatening situation and it is still fresh on your mind. But his friend knew that if he didn't face his fears and overcome them, he might not ever fly again. And if we don't face our giants of fear, we may never "fly in life" again, so to speak, either. We will live out our lives grounded, trying to serve the Lord and be faithful to Him, but never really flying high in the full plans and purposes of God.

2 Corinthians 10:4 mentions "weapons" and "warfare." You must realize that you are in a war, and demonic thoughts, ideas, and imaginations are the devil's weapons against you. Too many Christians are suffering from spiritual kinds of PTSDs that keep them grounded from flying victoriously in life.

Verse five tells us we need to destroy imaginations and speculations in our mind that don't agree with God's knowledge and truth. We must say like the Psalmist, "Search me, O God. Try me and know my anxious thoughts." When we know our anxious thoughts, we understand what we have to deal with, destroy, and then replace with God's thoughts of peace, love, and truth.

• •

Prayer Declaration – God, I thank You that You haven't given me a spirit of fear or timidity. I have Your Spirit of love, power, and a sound, healthy and peaceful mind. I thank You that I can and will control my thoughts. I will think and speak Your thoughts. I will take every thought captive and make it my slave to the truths and promises of Jesus Christ. Thank You, God.

Day 27

Uncovering Anxious Thoughts

Psalm 139:23 – "Search me, O God, and know my heart; try me and know <u>my</u> <u>anxious thoughts</u>."

If I'm struggling with timidity, worry, and fear, I can rest assured that I didn't get it from God. In fact, in the beginning, there was no timidity, worry, or fear in the world which the Lord had created for man. Fear and insecurity came after man foolishly listened to the devil and acted on his temptation and lie. Immediately after this, man became fearful and hid himself from God.

But thank God, Jesus came to restore our relationship with God. And now, through Christ, I have a spirit of love, power, and a sound, peaceful mind. I rebuke any spirit of fear, panic, or dread that may try to build on the property of my mind, in Jesus' name! I don't even want to allow for any timidity in my life. God's desire is for us to be filled with His confidence, joy, peace, and love. This is true mental health. This is walking in the mind of Christ. This is God's desire and plan for every one of His children.

I had struggled for several years with chronic fear, worry, and panic attacks that would come against me in certain situations. Sometimes when spending nights alone in the Chinese countryside, I'd have demonic attacks of fear wake me up or keep me from sleeping. Sometimes flying in small, cramped airplanes would bring on claustrophobic panic attacks that I would have to fight through.

The devil wanted to stop me from doing God's will for my life, and from enjoying my life as well. But the Lord wanted me to grow and learn how to overcome these battles. Our destinies in Christ are to be overcomers! That is your calling and God's plan for you.

• •

Prayer Declaration – Oh Lord, I trust You. I invite You to search me and know my thoughts. Reveal to me any wrong thoughts, any fearful worry-filled thoughts that aren't pleasing to You, or helpful to me. Then give me Your thoughts that I can use to fill and change that area of my thinking. Thank You that You cause me to have peace in my life, and serenity in my sleep.

Day 28

God Will Take Care Of You

1 Peter 5:7 – casting all your anxiety on Him, because He cares for you.

James C. Penny used to be a household name in America. Nowadays he is better known as J.C. Penny, the name of the clothing store chain that he started. Before he was fifty years old, Penny was a multimillionaire. He should have changed his last name from Penny to Millionaire.

Unfortunately, the stock market collapsed in 1929, and his Miami bank was forced to close on Christmas Eve of 1930. When it did, he lost millions.

At fifty-six, he had nothing left and became a poor man. If that wasn't bad enough, some people began to attack his character as well. Soon he ended up in the hospital with what today we might call a nervous breakdown.

He worried, "How will I be able to pay my hospital bill?" He was the man who had himself formerly endowed hospitals. That first night in the hospital was the blackest of Penny's life. He felt he would die before morning. So he lay down and waited to die. Instead of dying, he fell asleep and woke up the next morning finding that he was still alive.

Suddenly, from out in the hallway, he could hear an old song being sung. He followed the sound and heard:

Be not dismayed whate'er betide (whatever happens)*, God will take care of you.*

He finally found a group of people gathered to begin their day with God. He slipped into the hospital chapel, and the words "*whate'er betide*," "*whatever may happen*," echoed in his mind. He started to pray. "*Lord*," he cried, "*in myself, I can't do anything. Will you take care of me?*"

He said that somehow a weight was lifted from his spirit, and he came out of the room a different man. From that day on he often would repeat the words of the hymn: "*God will take care of me.*" As a result, as never before, he began to trust in God and find out God's plan for his life. He began to read the Bible and claim its promises afresh.

In time, he came out of his financial collapse and became wealthy again. He became an active Christian layman. The last part of his life was the best. He points to the morning in that hospital, when he made the quality decision to make God his senior partner, as the beginning of his success.

• •

Prayer Declaration – Lord, I thank You for Your promises. I give my cares, worries, and anxieties to You. They are no longer mine. I don't have a care. You care for me, my life, and my circumstances. I ask You to do what only You can do to answer my prayers, rescue me, and resolve my problems. Nothing is too difficult for You. Thank You for perfect peace.

Day 29

Don't Worry About Anything?

Philippians 4:6,7 - "Be anxious for nothing, but in everything by prayer and supplication with thanksgiving let your requests be made known to God.

7 And the peace of God, which surpasses all comprehension, will guard your hearts and your minds in Christ Jesus.

It seems that almost every Christian struggles with anxiety and fear about different issues of life. They are dealing with anxiety about their children, their marriage, their job or any number of things. I read about a bumper sticker that said, "If you aren't depressed, then you aren't paying attention." I think you could easily substitute the word "worried" for the word "depressed." Then it would read, "If you aren't *worried*, then you aren't paying attention." As you can see, it all depends on what you are paying attention to. The Bible tells us in Proverbs and Hebrews that we must pay close attention to the Lord and His Word if we expect to get God's blessings and results (**Hebrews 2:1; Proverbs 4:20-22**). We have to pay more attention to God's promises of peace and help if we want to experience His peace that passes understanding.

Paul is the one who wrote our Scripture meditation for today. He wrote it from prison! He is telling us that it's simply not God's will for us to ever have any anxiety in our lives about anything. In fact, He commands us not to. So what do we do when tempted to worry and feel anxious about things? We do what God's Word said to do. We must first pray about our problems, and then cast our anxiety and burden over on Him. But that is not all. Lastly, He tells us to *thank* Him for the answer. This is an essential part. When we thank Him, we are demonstrating that we believe He has heard our prayer and also is answering (has answered) our prayer.

And lastly, He leaves us with a plan to maintain the peace that we have received. We have to control what we think about and meditate on. If we control our thoughts and choose to meditate on the things that God instructs us to think upon, then we'll begin to find that anxiety and worries no longer find space in our minds. We have become filled with God's thoughts and God's peace. Remember, He cares for you. He calls you by name.

• •

Prayer Declaration – Lord, I thank You that You are the Prince of Peace and that one of the benefits of following You is a supernatural peace that passes all earthly understanding. Thank You that I don't have to carry my worries and fears. I can give them to You in prayer, and then You will work out the problems and set me free from anxiety.

Day 30

What To Do When Afraid

Psalm 56:3-4 "When I am afraid, I will put my trust in You.

4 In God, whose word I praise, In God I have put my trust; I shall not be afraid.

During the summer of 1992, my family and I were part of a team of over 90 people who traveled to Nizhny Novgorod, Russia to present a Music Festival and begin a new Russian church. It was a thrilling time of harvest and joy. We had the constant feeling of awe that we were in the midst of an historic move of God.

But after that first week, the bulk of the team left to return to America. After about two weeks, all but the long-term team was gone. And everyone else on our team had found an apartment except my family. We were still stuck in the negative 3-star (more like *black hole*) hotel, and were beginning to feel more and more isolated. We called our hotel the Mafia Hotel because of all the seedy individuals who seemed to be constantly flowing in and out of that place. My wife and I, along with our three small children, woke up each morning to a giant statue of Vladimir Ilyich Lenin outside our hotel room window that faced the square. His outstretched arm seemed to be pointing right at our window, and us! He was like a giant Goliath shouting every day, "Who do you think you are, coming into my territory? Now you are alone with me. Let's see how much faith you have. I'm gonna feed you and your family to the birds of the air, and send you running home with your tail between your legs."

Spiritually it was an exciting and awesome time, seeing so many people getting saved at the meetings. But that wasn't happening at the hotel! And there was no restaurant in the hotel. We had to search for food every day. We had to wash our clothes in the tub. The reality of living in the former Soviet Union, with what seemed like an almost collapsed economy, was not easy by any means. Drunken people staggered around every day. Desperate men and women were breaking out in fistfights as they struggled to find basic necessities. It was a wild and sometimes scary time. We prayed, trusted the Lord, and He protected us. Finally, after six long weeks, we were able to move out of the hotel and into our own apartment. Praise God!

In **Psalm 56** David tells us what he said when he was afraid. He would often say, "When I am afraid, I will put my trust in You. I shall not be afraid." We need to say these words out loud to ourselves and believe them!

• •

Prayer Declaration – Lord, I thank You that my heart doesn't have to stay troubled. In times of fear, I say like David, "…I trust in You, Lord, and the promises of Your Word. I'm not afraid anymore." By Your grace, I have peace. By Your grace I *smile at the future* (**Proverbs 31:25**).

Day 31

Rescue In The Day Of Trouble

Psalm 50:15 – (NAS) "Call upon Me in the day of trouble; I shall rescue you, and you will honor Me."

NLT – "Then call on me when you are in trouble, and I will rescue you, and you will give me glory."

August 31, 1955, Christy Wilson, missionary to Afghanistan, glanced at his watch and immediately knew something was wrong. They should have been preparing to land by now. He peered out of the Iran Air DC 3 window, and seeing forests, suddenly realized they were lost! Kabul, their destination, was at least one hundred miles from the nearest forest.

Two Americans were at the controls of the plane. The pilot had never been in Afghanistan, and the co-pilot, who was the navigator, was only on his second flight in the country! They were flying without the aid of sophisticated navigational equipment that is used today.

Somewhere during the flight, they had made a wrong turn. Christy swallowed hard and saw there was no place to land anywhere among the jagged Central Asian wilderness. Soon the twilight disappeared, and an endless sea of blackness engulfed them. The more he thought about it, the more he realized the next few hours could very well be his last on earth.

Christy was allowed to go into the cockpit. He told the pilots he was a minister. The co-pilot glanced over his shoulder and said, "Use all the influence you have." He answered, "I'm praying, and I know God is in charge." The pilot then made a 180-degree bank left and headed back to Kandahar. He returned to his seat and began to pray more. He placed the fifteen people on the plane in God's hands. Then he pulled out his Bible and wrote a final note to his family on the inside cover. If they crashed, maybe the Bible would be found.

He finished signing the note when from the corner of his eye he saw a full moon rising. God gave them a full moon miracle in a clear sky at just the right time! He went back to the cockpit and scouted the landscape below. Quickly he recognized the village of Qalat. They checked the map, found their location, and headed for Kandahar. God had answered his prayers.

Just over an hour later they began to see the glow of Kandahar in the distance. But they still faced a major problem. They couldn't land because the airport runway had no lights.

When they reached the outskirts of Kandahar, Christy sighted the Morrison-Knutsen Construction camp. "Fly low over the camp," he suggested, "and maybe the noise of the engines will attract attention, and the workers will find a way to help us."

The pilots made three low passes, and within minutes, many vehicles were racing to the airfield. Their lights flooded the runway, and the plane was able to make a perfect landing.

Never before had Christy been so grateful for answered prayer. Our Scripture for today, **Psalm 50:15**, came to his mind. He thanked God for the promise that for those who "call on Him in their time of trouble," He will "rescue them and they will give Him glory." ("More to be Desired Than Gold," Christy Wilson. P. 109-113)

• •

Prayer Declaration – Lord, I thank You that the words You have spoken bring blessed peace. I call on You and You rescue me. I won't allow fear to get control of my life. Together, we will overcome the challenges I face today, in Jesus' name. Praise God!

Made in the USA
Coppell, TX
20 March 2021

52022331R00049